NO MORE MORE WORRIES!

NO MORE WORRIES!

An Hachette UK Company
www.hachette.co.uk

Vie Books, an imprint of Summersdale Publishers Ltd
Part of Octopus Publishing Group Limited
Carmelite House
50 Victoria Embankment
LONDON
EC4Y 0DZ
UK

www.summersdale.com

Printed and bound in China

ISBN: 978-1-78783-935-9

Substantial discounts on bulk quantities of Summersdale books are available to corporations, professional associations and other organizations. For details contact general enquiries: telephone: +44 (0) 1243 771107 or email: enquiries@summersdale.com.

NO MORE WORRIES!

Outsmart Anxiety and Be Positively You

POPPY O'NEILL

vie

CONTENTS

FOREWORD

It seems as if there has never been a more important time for us to be focusing on the mental health of young people than the present. In the past year, as a result of lockdowns, young people have experienced a number of different factors that have come together to have a significant impact on their mental health. These have included isolation from friends, disruption of normal routines and increased stress trying to keep up with their education online. All of these factors have led to a dramatic increase in teen anxiety and mental health problems and referrals to increasingly stretched mental health services.

This new book from Poppy O'Neill, the latest in a series of resources aimed at supporting the mental health of children and young people is a welcome addition to help teenagers and their families understand and manage their increasing levels of anxiety.

One of the strengths of *No More Worries!* is that it combines a wealth of information with a highly accessible style. The book begins with a comprehensive overview of what anxiety is, how anxiety holds us back, and allows teenagers to become aware of exactly how their anxiety manifests. The real strength of this book lies in the subsequent chapters, which outline a wide range of strategies to help a young person manage their anxiety. These include such diverse topics as mindfulness, journaling, and appropriate expression of feelings.

As a mental health professional myself, I was particularly pleased to see a chapter emphasising the importance of self-care, an area that in my experience can be all too easily overlooked by many. This chapter includes sound advice on exercise, diet and sleep, areas that many of us might not immediately associate with improving our mental health, but are vital nonetheless.

I would highly recommend this book and hope that it serves its purpose in helping empower teenagers to understand, manage and overcome their anxiety.

Graham Kennedy MA, UKCP Reg
Integrative Child & Adolescent Psychotherapist
Attachment and Trauma Consultant

April 2021

INTRODUCTION

Welcome to *No More Worries!*, a guide to understanding and taming anxiety so you can live your best life.

When you're a teen, you go through so many changes and challenges, both inside and out. Your brain develops at a super-fast rate, transforming the way you think and experience the world. This means you're full of potential, and capable of learning and achieving great things, but on the flip side you can also feel more stressed and anxious. Friendships, puberty, relationships, exam stress, social media, peer pressure and family drama can make it difficult to feel calm and in control of your emotions. On the surface, it seems that everyone else is breezing through teenage life, but speak to anyone and you'll soon be reassured that this isn't the case.

Using a mix of ideas, activities and proven techniques used by therapists – like cognitive behavioural therapy (CBT) and mindfulness – this book will help you to shift how you see your emotions and think about the challenges you face and, most importantly, show you how to feel positive every day.

IT'S OK NOT TO BE OK

Anxiety sucks. It's like a dark cloud holding you back from living life to the full. When you're feeling anxious, it can get really lonely, but you're not the only one experiencing this.

Everyone feels anxiety – it's just that everyone hides it slightly differently. The funny thing is, the more we feel alone and ashamed of our feelings, the more important it is to share them.

It's OK to struggle. It's OK to ask for help. It's OK to need reassurance or support or just a listening ear. It's OK to cry or feel angry or need space. The way you feel is always valid. You are not a burden; you are a human being. There are people in your life who care about you and want to know about your thoughts, feelings and challenges. They'll want to hear what's on your mind, and what they can do to help.

You are allowed to be exactly as you are right now. There's no need to do anything more than accept yourself. The truth is that life is both terrifying and beautiful, and you don't need to have it all figured out in order to enjoy it.

WHAT THIS BOOK WILL DO FOR YOU

This book will help you understand how your mind and emotions work, and how anxiety affects your whole body. You'll learn how to harness your strength so that anxiety doesn't become the boss of you.

The more you learn about yourself, the greater confidence you'll have in managing your thoughts and feelings. So if you're struggling with anxiety and sick of it controlling your life, you've come to the right place.

You already have all the tools and potential inside of you to beat anxiety, and this book will help you to uncover them. So read on and remember: you have the power to outsmart anxiety and be positively you.

HOW TO USE THIS BOOK

This book is for you if...

★ **You often feel nervous, worried or afraid.**

★ **You have troubling, recurring thoughts.**

★ **You need a lot of reassurance to feel OK.**

★ **You struggle to get to sleep.**

★ **You feel ill or exhausted because of anxiety.**

★ **You feel anxious about aspects of your body, identity or personality.**

★ **You keep quiet about your desires, needs and opinions.**

★ **You get anxious in social situations.**

★ **You struggle to find your voice.**

If that sounds like you sometimes, or even all the time, this book is here to help. The effect that anxiety has on your life can be reduced significantly and you have the power to change your outlook for the better.

Inside these pages you'll find all sorts of advice on how to keep calm and cope with anxiety. You'll learn strategies to help you face your fears and feel more comfortable with your emotions.

This book is about you, so take it at your own pace. Some of the ideas will be useful and others not so much, and it's completely OK to go with what feels right for you.

PART 1:

ANXIETY AND YOU

WHAT IS ANXIETY?

Anxiety is a response to danger that evolved in humans tens of thousands of years ago. In prehistoric times, threats could come from wild animals, natural disasters, illness and lack of food or shelter. When our brains sense danger, they send signals throughout the whole body via the nervous system, telling us that it's time to act.

This whole-body response is often called "fight or flight", but the most up-to-date research has found that we can also freeze or do what therapist and author Pete Walker calls "fawn". These words describe the different ways in which we act when we're feeling overwhelming anxiety.

When danger might have come from a sabre-toothed tiger, and being outcast from your friends or family could mean starvation, these responses were super-useful and helped human beings learn how to survive and thrive. There are still real dangers out there, and feeling fear or anxiety helps to keep us safe in the modern world, too.

Our brain's main job is to protect us, but it sometimes still perceives danger as if we were stuck in prehistoric times. Anything that might make us feel difficult emotions can appear as dangerous to the brain, causing it to send out anxiety signals around the body. This is why we can feel anxious about things that we know, logically, won't harm us.

Fight: the urge to attack.

Flight: the urge to run away.

Freeze: the feeling of being rooted to the spot.

Fawn: the urge to calm others down.

HOW TO SPOT ANXIOUS THOUGHTS

When you're having a hard time, anxious thoughts can feel like they're just the truth. How can you spot when anxiety is driving your thoughts? Luckily, there are a few clues that can help you. Anxiety likes to paint the most negative, disastrous, dramatic picture of the world that it possibly can, so watch out for these dead giveaways:

Always
e.g. *I always fail!*

Never
e.g. *this will never end!*

Everyone
e.g. *everyone hates me!*

No one
e.g. *no one appreciates me!*

Should
e.g. *I should be different!*

Making up stories
e.g. *the world is against me and I am powerless to change anything about my life!*

When you catch yourself thinking like this, be kind to yourself. It's OK and you haven't done anything wrong. We all get caught up in anxious thoughts sometimes. The trick is to recognize them and understand that they are not true.

EVERYONE EXPERIENCES A VERSION OF ANXIETY OR WORRY IN THEIR LIVES.

Emma Stone

WHAT ANXIETY FEELS LIKE

Anxiety feels different for everybody. But these are some of the most common signs that we're feeling anxious:

Racing thoughts

Really thirsty

Coughing

Loss of appetite

Dry mouth

Craving sugar

Dizziness

Nausea

Can't keep still

Urge to fight back

Difficulty speaking

Stomach ache

Shyness

I FEEL

Frozen to the spot

Urge to hide

Needing to go to the toilet

Shallow breathing

Too hot or too cold

Urge to run away

Racing heart

Difficulty speaking your mind

Sweating

Urge to blame others

Hard to keep eye contact

Anxiety can make us behave differently, too. This is because feeling anxious is really uncomfortable, and our minds want to make those feelings stop! Here are some of the things anxiety can make us do:

★ **Ask for reassurance**

★ **Run away**

★ **Hide**

★ **Lash out**

★ **Keep silent**

★ **Flatter the other person**

★ **Cling to others**

★ **Blame other people**

★ **Keep very busy**

★ **Stay in bed**

★ **Jiggle around**

★ **Nail biting**

★ **Lip chewing**

★ **Rub or scratch your skin**

★ **Cry**

WHAT DOES ANXIETY FEEL AND LOOK LIKE FOR YOU?

Think of a time recently when you felt anxious, worried or afraid. What did that feel like in your body? What did you do? Write it below – you can use the examples on the previous page and add your own.

Thinking about and writing down how anxiety feels for you will help you to spot it in future. When you can recognize anxiety, it becomes easier to deal with.

YOU DON'T HAVE TO STRUGGLE IN SILENCE. YOU CAN BE UN-SILENT.

Demi Lovato

ALL ABOUT ME

Let's take some time to get to know you! The better you know yourself, the stronger you are. Here are some prompts to get you thinking – jot down your answers here or on another piece of paper if you feel like writing more!

My name is...

I'm excellent at...

My perfect day would be...

If I could change one thing about my life, it would be...

If I knew I couldn't fail, I'd...

My dream job is...

I'm really glad I...

Recently, I learned...

I'm excited for...

My worst fear is...

I feel good when I...

If I want to relax, I...

WHAT DO YOUNG PEOPLE WORRY ABOUT?

You're not alone in feeling anxious. Everyone worries, and you can't tell how anxious someone is, or why, just from looking at them. Here are some of the things young people your age most commonly worry about:

- ★ **Adulthood**
- ★ **Appearance**
- ★ **Social media**
- ★ **Popularity**
- ★ **Weight**
- ★ **Relationships**

- ★ **Friendships**
- ★ **Family issues**
- ★ **Schoolwork**
- ★ **Health**
- ★ **Puberty**

Some of these things might be relatable, while others might seem like no big deal. Perhaps what brings you anxiety isn't on this list. Our minds are very complicated things and everyone is different.

THERE IS NO STANDARD NORMAL. NORMAL IS SUBJECTIVE. THERE ARE SEVEN BILLION VERSIONS OF NORMAL ON THIS PLANET.

Matt Haig

HOW ANXIETY CAN HOLD YOU BACK

Anxiety can get in the way of all sorts of things: it's different for everybody and, however you experience it, you're not alone. Here are some common ways in which anxiety affects young people.

I wish I could hang out with my friends more, but the thought of embarrassing myself makes me too anxious.

I worry a lot about not being perfect, so I put off starting school projects until the very last minute.

Any time I get a cough or feel an ache, I worry that I have a serious illness. But I feel too worried to go to the doctor or talk to my parents about it.

A few years ago, my uncle was in a car accident. He's OK now but the thought of someone in my family being in an accident keeps me up at night.

I really didn't want to watch a horror movie last Halloween, but I was too scared of being dumped by my friends so I didn't say anything. I had nightmares for weeks after watching it and I wish I'd had the confidence to be honest with them.

I worry a lot about food, and I think about it all the time. It's exhausting! I have all these rules about what and when I can eat. It feels like something bad will happen if I stop thinking about it.

MY ANXIETY

What makes you feel anxious? Perhaps it's a thought that keeps you awake at night or a situation you go out of your way to avoid. It might be one particular thing or a whole bunch of things. Writing it all down is a bit like downloading files to an external hard drive – it frees up space in your head! If you find it difficult to put it into words, try instead to draw the things that worry you. Write or draw as many as you can think of here:

PANIC ATTACKS

Sometimes anxiety gets so overwhelming that you feel completely out of control. This is called a panic attack. During a panic attack, you might feel dizzy, hot and unwell; your heart beats faster and it can be difficult to catch a breath.

If you ever feel like you're having a panic attack, here are some things you can do to help you cope until it passes:

★ **Ask for help from someone you trust – they could sit with you, hug you or hold your hand.**

★ **Close your eyes.**

★ **Remember that the panic attack will end soon, and that it can't hurt you.**

★ **Think about your breathing – count to four as you breathe in, then out for four, and repeat.**

★ **Once the panic attack has passed, be very gentle with yourself. You might feel tired or thirsty, or you might want to move around, or get some fresh air. Listen to your body and go slowly.**

Although panic attacks feel really distressing and frightening, they can't hurt you. It is simply the feeling of your brain and nervous system setting off an emergency alarm in your body, causing you to feel that "fight, flight, freeze or fawn" sense of danger.

PART 2:
DEALING WITH ANXIETY

HOW TO DEAL WITH ANXIETY

So now you know a bit more about what anxiety is and how to recognize it, what can you do about it? Firstly, it's important to remember that everyone feels a bit anxious, some of the time. That becomes a problem when it gets in the way of you living your life. So if anxiety stops you from getting enough sleep, doing the things you love and being yourself, then it makes sense to learn some skills that will help you to feel less anxious. In this chapter we'll look at strategies for calming anxiety fast.

WRITE IT OUT

What's on your mind? In the previous section you wrote about all the things that cause you anxiety. Now it's time to focus on the one thing that's bugging you at this very moment.

There's plenty of room, so keep writing all your thoughts about it here... You can carry on, using another piece of paper, if you run out of space.

I keep thinking about the time...

I'm nervous about...

I wish I didn't have to...

I worry that...

Writing down your worries is a great way to start dealing with them. It's like uploading anxious thoughts from your mind onto a piece of paper, freeing up your headspace for something else.

CALM BRAIN vs ANXIOUS BRAIN

What's it like in your brain when you feel calm? What kinds of things do you think about? What colour or pattern might represent your mood?

Write, draw and colour in your calm brain here:

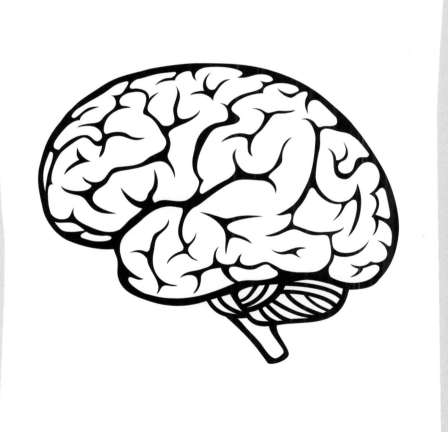

What's it like in your mind when you're feeling anxious? Perhaps it's taken up with just one thought or image, or maybe there are lots. Use words, pictures and colours to illustrate your anxious brain here:

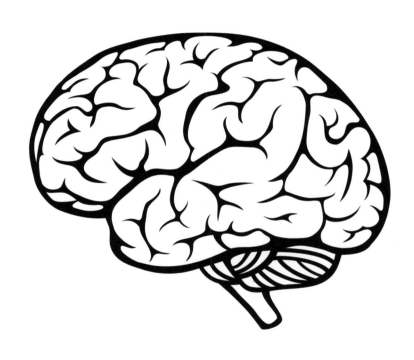

Your calm brain and your anxious brain probably look quite different now you've filled them in. The way we feel in our mind and nervous system influences our whole outlook on life. When anxiety becomes really overwhelming, it can be difficult to think about anything else.

DON'T LET THAT FEAR HOLD YOU. DON'T LET IT HOLD YOU ANY MORE.

Karamo Brown

LISTEN TO YOUR BODY AND MIND

When you feel anxious, that sensation comes from the part of your brain that controls emotions: the amygdala. If your brain senses danger (even if it's not really a dangerous situation, just something you're worried about, like an exam), the amygdala sends feelings of anxiety all around your body.

When you start to feel anxiety building, don't try to stop the feeling or pretend it's not there. Instead, take a deep breath and talk yourself through the sensation, a bit like this:

★ **I'm feeling anxiety.**

★ **I'm safe: feelings can't hurt me.**

★ **What is the anxiety trying to tell me?**

★ **It's telling me that I might fail this exam, my parents will be disappointed and I might never get a good job.**

★ **That might happen: I don't know the future. If it happens, I'll cope. I can't control other people's emotions.**

★ **I can describe the feeling in my body – I feel hot and my heart is beating fast.**

★ **I am safe to feel this and to think these thoughts. This will pass.**

While simply sitting with the feelings and thoughts that anxiety brings you is enough, it can also be helpful to learn some techniques that will help them pass more quickly. Read on for some great anxiety-soothing recommendations.

MINDFUL BREATHING

Mindfulness means paying attention to the present moment. It's a concept that originated in Buddhist philosophy and it's been proven to reduce anxiety, improve concentration and boost self-esteem. You can do almost anything mindfully – eating, working, stroking a pet... All you need to do is focus all your attention on the activity. So if you're cuddling your dog mindfully, you notice the smell and texture of its fur, the warmth of its body and the emotions you feel. When you do this, your mind doesn't have time to focus on anxious thoughts.

Mindful breathing is a great skill to learn because it's always available to you, wherever you are and whatever you're doing. Here's how:

Take a deep breath in through your nose. Feel the air flowing through your nostrils. Notice your chest and belly expand. Breathe out and feel your body relax, noticing how the air feels as it flows out of your nostrils – is it warmer or cooler than the in-breath? Breathe in again and keep going like this for three breaths, or for however long you need.

ALTERNATE NOSTRIL BREATHING

This is another powerful breathing technique that you can use to calm your nervous system in a hurry. Place your fingers against the sides of your nose and use them to control your breath so that you are forced to concentrate on your breathing. This takes your attention away from anxious thoughts, while the increased oxygen delivered to your bloodstream from deep breathing calms your body.

Here's how to do it:

First, use one finger to squish down your right nostril.

Take a deep breath in through your left nostril.

Hold your breath while you release your right nostril, swap hands and squish down your left nostril.

Breathe out through your right nostril.

Now do it again, but this time the other way round.

Keep going for five breaths, or until you're ready to stop.

MOVEMENT

Moving your body helps difficult emotions to move through you. It doesn't really matter what type of activity you choose, but studies have found that rhythmic movement is best for calming the nervous system and reducing anxiety.

Dancing

Letting your body move in time to music releases feel-good brain chemicals, as well as getting rid of anxious energy. Singing along at top volume doubles the benefits, because it makes your chest and throat vibrate, soothing your nervous system. Try sticking on your favourite song and dancing like no one's watching.

Yoga

Stretching into yoga poses releases tension in your body and helps to improve your ability to tolerate uncomfortable sensations – making it easier for you to cope with anxiety. Yoga also helps you relax, slows your breathing and releases endorphins in your brain. Check online for some simple yoga poses to try.

Walking

Walking off anxiety really works. The rhythm of your footsteps calms your amygdala and nervous system, because rhythmic movement signals to this part of your brain that you are safe. Try walking around the block or going for a family stroll in your nearest park.

Moving intuitively

This simply means listening to your body and seeing how it wants to move, and what it needs. You might find yourself swaying, stretching or even making noises. This one's best to try when you're alone, so you don't worry about what anyone else thinks!

Bouncing

A trampoline is a brilliant place to calm your anxiety. If you don't have one, bouncing on your heels, rocking or jumping on the spot will have a similar effect. Just like walking, the rhythmic movement will calm your mind and body.

Feel-good brain chemicals

These are dopamine, oxytocin, serotonin and endorphins.

Dopamine causes the short-lived feeling of satisfaction when you achieve something, like completing a task, getting a social media "like" or catching a ball.

Oxytocin gives us that warm, fuzzy feeling that comes from physical contact, like hugs or stroking a pet.

Serotonin is released when we get recognition or admiration from others, such as winning an award or being praised for some hard work.

Endorphins are released to help us cope with pain, and they keep us going when we might otherwise want to give up – they help you to complete a run and cause that elated feeling you get after a cold swim.

HOW BIG IS MY PROBLEM?

Anxiety can keep us frozen. When you're caught up in anxious thoughts, problems can feel bigger than they truly are. Take a moment to bring your thoughts back down to earth, by thinking logically about how big your problem is.

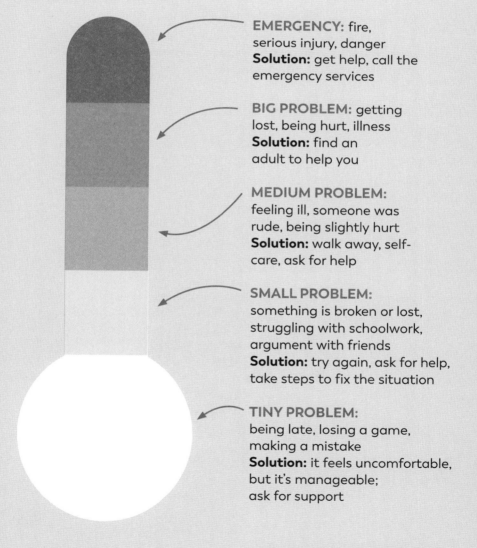

EMERGENCY: fire, serious injury, danger
Solution: get help, call the emergency services

BIG PROBLEM: getting lost, being hurt, illness
Solution: find an adult to help you

MEDIUM PROBLEM: feeling ill, someone was rude, being slightly hurt
Solution: walk away, self-care, ask for help

SMALL PROBLEM: something is broken or lost, struggling with schoolwork, argument with friends
Solution: try again, ask for help, take steps to fix the situation

TINY PROBLEM: being late, losing a game, making a mistake
Solution: it feels uncomfortable, but it's manageable; ask for support

Even with a tiny problem, you can ask for help. It's OK if your feelings are bigger than the issue. Using a scale like this will help you to work out if there are any steps you can take to solve the problem and lessen your anxiety.

Sometimes you might feel anxiety that doesn't come from a real-life situation or problem – like worrying that something you saw on the news might happen to you or your family. You can still use this scale to consider how you might respond if you were in that situation.

ANXIETY DIARY

Understanding your relationship with anxiety will help you to bring it under control. It's a good idea to keep an anxiety diary so you can make a note of what makes you feel high anxiety, how it feels for you and, crucially, what helps to calm you in these moments.

Keep a record of every time you feel anxious and see if you can learn something from each one.

Date:

What caused the anxious feeling?

What did it feel like?

What thoughts did you have?

Did you try any strategies?

What helped?

What didn't help?

Date:

What caused the anxious feeling?

What did it feel like?

What thoughts did you have?

Did you try any strategies?

What helped?

What didn't help?

Date:

What caused the anxious feeling?

What did it feel like?

What thoughts did you have?

Did you try any strategies?

What helped?

What didn't help?

Date:

What caused the anxious feeling?

What did it feel like?

What thoughts did you have?

Did you try any strategies?

What helped?

What didn't help?

Date:

What caused the anxious feeling?

What did it feel like?

What thoughts did you have?

Did you try any strategies?

What helped?

What didn't help?

SCARED IS WHAT YOU'RE FEELING. BRAVE IS WHAT YOU'RE DOING.

Emma Donoghue

THINGS YOU CAN CONTROL... AND THINGS YOU CAN'T

When you're feeling anxious, it's easy to forget what is within your control and what isn't. When something is outside of your control, no amount of anxiety will change it. When something is within your control, you have the power to take action and change it for the better.

THOUGHTS, FEELINGS AND ACTIONS

How we think, how we feel and how we act are all linked. For example, someone who thinks they'll make a mistake and be laughed at if they speak up in class will feel very anxious when they need to ask a question at school, and they'll end up keeping quiet and not finding an answer.

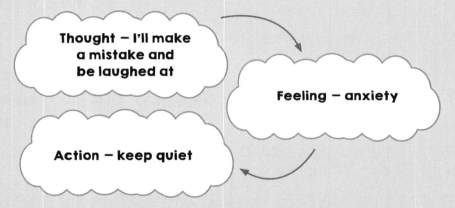

Everyone has different thoughts and feelings, which is why we all act differently. Here's how someone else might think, feel and act in a similar situation:

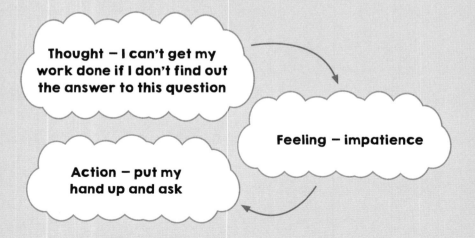

Can you remember a time when you felt anxious? Check back in your anxiety diary on page 43 to remind yourself of a specific situation.

Can you work out how your thoughts influenced your feelings, and your feelings influenced your actions?

Thought

Feeling

Action

CHANGE YOUR THOUGHTS

We've learned that thoughts influence feelings, and feelings influence actions. So it makes sense that if you think different thoughts, you'll be able to take more control over your feelings and be able to choose different actions.

Just like a funny joke will only make you laugh for a certain length of time, but you might think of it and laugh again days later... in the same way, anxious thoughts bring anxious feelings and memories.

Changing your thoughts begins with the knowledge that they are not facts: they're stories that we can choose to believe or not... And many of them have massive plot holes.

We call these plot holes "thinking errors" – let's take a look at the most common types.

Focus on the negatives: that's all I can see – even when something nice happens, I always find a way to feel bad about it.

All-or-nothing thinking: if something isn't perfect, I've failed completely.

Catastrophizing: if a small, bad thing happens, it'll ruin everything.

Mind-reading: I know what other people are thinking about me.

Fortune-telling: I know something will go wrong.

Feelings are facts: I feel like a failure, so I'll definitely fail.

Putting yourself down: I'm useless – I can't do anything.

Perfectionism: I should be perfect at everything. I should never make a mistake or need help.

BLAMING: IT'S ALL MY/THEIR FAULT!

Do any of these thinking errors sound familiar? Perhaps you think like this sometimes, or a lot of the time. Can you work out what's wrong with each one? Some of them are being really unfair to yourself, while others involve predicting the future.

But when you're stuck thinking like this, it can feel very real. The best thing to do is talk it all through with a trusted friend or adult. Quite often, this helps to understand where the thoughts could be untrue. In the next chapter, we'll look in detail at how to change your thinking habits so you can use your mind to help calm your anxiety.

NOTHING IS WRONG - WHATEVER IS HAPPENING IS JUST "REAL LIFE".

Tara Brach

PART 3:

HOW TO TAKE CONTROL

LEARNING TO CONTROL YOUR ANXIETY

In the last chapter we learned about different ways to calm anxious thoughts and feelings in your mind and body. The key to managing anxiety in the long term is to learn to recognize the moment it begins to take hold. When you can see anxiety for what it is – just thoughts and emotions – you are more able to cope with it, and it will pass more quickly.

The more you prove to and remind yourself that you're strong and capable, even when you feel anxious, the less your anxiety will be able to control you.

CALMING YOUR NERVOUS SYSTEM

Remember all the different types of anxiety-reducing movement on page 39? They are all good ways of calming the nervous system but now it's time to have a think about what works for *your* nervous system. Everyone is totally unique and one person's calming movement might feel quite stressful for somebody else.

Below are some other activities that can be soothing for the nervous system. Perhaps you'll recognize one or two that you've always found strangely relaxing, but you've never realized why before...

* **Singing**

* **Humming**

* **Household chores**

* **Splashing your face with cold water**

* **Taking a cold shower**

* **Reading aloud**

* **Laughing**

* **Hugging**

* **Using a weighted blanket**

* **Drumming**

* **Massage**

* **Breathing exercises**

Knowing what manages to calm your nervous system is the first step towards building your resilience to anxiety, as you'll be aware of what to do when anxiety strikes.

What works to calm your nervous system? Choose from the list on the previous page and add your own ideas here:

AFFIRMATIONS

An affirmation is a short, positive sentence that is designed to help you feel better, calmer, more confident and compassionate toward yourself. They're best said out loud, in front of a mirror, but you can think or say them to yourself any time, anywhere!

Once your body starts to feel calmer, it's useful to have an affirmation that works well to soothe your anxious thoughts. The more you repeat a certain positive phrase, the more powerful it will be against anxiety. This is because each time you think something, the brain believes it that bit more. So replacing anxious thoughts with positive affirmations weakens your negative beliefs, while strengthening the new, positive ones. Try incorporating an affirmation or two into your morning routine.

Again, what works for you will be unique to you. Here are a bunch of ideas for anxiety-soothing affirmations. You can use any of these as they are, adapt them or make up your own:

★ I'm safe.

★ The world is a kind place.

★ As I relax, anxiety flows out of me.

★ I am capable of anything.

★ I can do this.

★ One step at a time.

★ I can do the next right thing.

★ I am brave.

★ I am in control.

★ This will pass.

★ I trust myself.

★ I have everything I need.

★ I can cope.

★ I trust the process.

★ I can go with the flow.

★ I can say "no".

★ I feel centred.

★ This is temporary.

★ I accept myself as I am.

★ I love myself.

★ I am not afraid.

★ I am not alone.

★ I am loved.

- ★ I can do my best.
- ★ However tall the mountain, I can climb it.
- ★ I am not in danger.
- ★ Things are working out in my favour.
- ★ I am allowed to make mistakes.
- ★ I let go of what I cannot control.
- ★ I am safe to feel this.

Write your own ideas for affirmations here:

WHAT DOES YOUR ANXIETY LOOK LIKE?

Can you picture what your anxiety would look like if it were in front of you? Perhaps it would be a person, an animal or a monster, or a colour or shape? With the help of your imagination, create a picture of your anxiety. You can use paint, pens or pencils, whatever you have at hand...

Creating an image of your anxiety helps you to separate yourself from it. You are more than what you think and feel at any given moment, and anxiety is simply something that visits you sometimes.

FACTS AND OPINIONS

Anxiety can often make opinions seem like facts. Here's an example:

Fact: I got a low grade for my last English assignment.

Opinion: I'll always fail, whatever I try.

Anxiety takes a fact and twists it into a thinking error (in this example it's a mixture of "fortune-telling", "catastrophizing" and "putting yourself down").

It's actually really hard for our minds to just leave a fact alone and not make an opinion out of it! So instead, try to find the lesson, like this:

Fact: I got a low grade for my last English assignment.

Opinion: I feel disappointed. That assignment was difficult for me and I can learn from this. I bet I'll do better next time.

See how the fact doesn't change, but the opinion is so much more positive?

Now it's your turn. Can you think of a fact that brings you anxiety? Perhaps it's something that happened to you or someone you know, and you're worried about it happening again. Or perhaps it's something you have coming up in the future and you're not sure how it'll go.

Write it here...

Fact:

Now think about an anxious opinion that your mind has invented from this fact...

Opinion:

Can you think of an alternative opinion that could replace it? It might be positive, like: "I'll do really well..." or neutral, such as: "I can't know how it will turn out" – whichever works for you.

REFRAMING

What you did in the last exercise is called "reframing". It's a powerful technique used by therapists and psychologists to show that there is always a calmer or more positive way of looking at any situation.

Here are some more useful things to ask yourself to help re-frame anxious thoughts:

What advice would I give my best friend in this situation?

What would someone with high self-esteem do in this situation?

What advice would a wise, calm and peaceful person give to me?

Can I make this thought 10 per cent kinder to myself?

What if this thought is just a thought, and I don't need to do anything about it?

What would a positive outcome look like?

What would a neutral outcome look like?

COURAGE IS FOUND IN UNLIKELY PLACES.

J. R. R. Tolkien

USING MINDFULNESS TO BEAT ANXIETY

Remember we learned about mindfulness on page 37? When you're feeling anxious, you're often very concerned with what might happen in the future, so mindfulness can be really helpful. It focuses your mind on what is going on right now and reminds you that you can handle this moment.

Here's a mindfulness exercise for when you need to distract yourself from anxiety.

Mindful feet

Sit or stand – whichever is more comfortable, as long as your feet are touching the ground. Think about the soles of your feet. You don't need to look at them: just bring your mind's attention to them.

What can the soles of your feet feel? What sensations, temperatures and textures are you aware of?

Think about the tips of your toes, and then slowly move your attention along the bottom of your feet until you get to your heel.

That's it! Thinking very hard about the soles of your feet means that your mind can't be taken up with anxious thoughts, as it's too busy being in the moment.

BREAKING THE WORRY CYCLE

Anxious thoughts can go round and round in your head, leading to other worries and new imagined scenarios, before circling back to the origin of your anxiety. Argh! It's easy to get stuck in a thought spiral.

It's like anxiety is constantly reminding you of all the things that could go wrong, just in case you forget for one millisecond.

So how can you break the cycle? Anxious thought spirals are very hard to ignore. Often, the answer is to listen.

Try writing down all the thoughts that anxiety is bringing into your mind, no matter how unlikely they might seem:

(You could also tell a trusted friend or adult what you're thinking.)

Can you see how your anxiety is trying to keep you safe? Even if it gets a bit (or a lot) carried away sometimes, your brain's number-one job is to protect you from danger.

Now try saying out loud, in your head or in writing:

"Thank you, anxiety, I'll keep that in mind."

Writing down and acknowledging the possibilities that your anxious brain has imagined will make it feel easier to let them go from your mind.

JOURNALING

Writing down your anxious thoughts is a brilliant habit to get into. Not only is it a great way to let them out of your mind, but it also helps you to choose different, calmer thoughts and ideas to replace them with.

Writing in a diary or journal before bed each night can help you to fall asleep more easily. You don't need anything fancy to get started – any notebook will work.

You can simply write down your thoughts – or try this everyday bedtime journaling exercise:

Something that's troubling me:

What I would say to myself or do if I wasn't afraid:

Journaling can be really helpful. It's also a great idea to talk through any worries or problems you have with someone you trust.

YOU ARE OK EXACTLY AS YOU ARE

There's a lot in this book about lowering anxiety and having more control over anxious thoughts, and it might feel like you should be quickly seeing changes or improvements... You might even feel anxious about still feeling anxious!

No matter what, you will always have ups and downs in life. It's OK to go at your own pace – things take as long as they take, and your emotional well-being is not a race or a competition. It's OK to be exactly where you are, and it's very, very OK to find this difficult.

Learning about your mind and emotions, and applying that knowledge to your thoughts and feelings *is* difficult. You can take things one step at a time, and you can also take a step back, retrace your steps or stand still for a while. It gets easier when you take the pressure off.

TRUST YOURSELF

Anxiety usually strikes because we fear not being in control. For example, you are likely to feel anxious in social situations because you have no power over what others think about you, and that can seem really threatening. You might try to have some control over it by not really being yourself when you're around others – whether that's by keeping very quiet, telling lots of jokes or something else.

The antidote to feeling the need to control everything is to build trust – in other people but also, especially, in yourself.

When you trust yourself, you value your own opinion of yourself more than other people's. You trust that you can ask for help if you need it, and you know that you'll cope, even if things don't go quite the way you planned.

The good news is that you're already building up your self-trust. Every time you choose a kind, patient, positive or calm thought over an anxious one, you believe a little more that your mind can be a gentle, supportive place. Every time you take the time to listen to your body and help yourself relax, you trust in your resilience a little more.

KEEP A PROMISE TO YOURSELF

A great way to build up self-trust is to make a promise to yourself and keep it for a week. Choose something small and achievable like: "I promise to drink a glass of water first thing every morning for a week."

Make keeping the promise as easy as possible – for example, make sure you have a drink of water by your bed before you go to sleep, so it's there for you first thing. If you miss a day, don't be hard on yourself – just remember that you can keep the promise the next day.

What promise will you make to yourself this week?

PROMISE TRACKER

Keep track of your promise to yourself here.

☐ **Monday**

☐ **Tuesday**

☐ **Wednesday**

☐ **Thursday**

☐ **Friday**

☐ **Saturday**

☐ **Sunday**

DON'T TRY TO WIN OVER THE HATERS; YOU ARE NOT A JACKASS WHISPERER.

Brené Brown

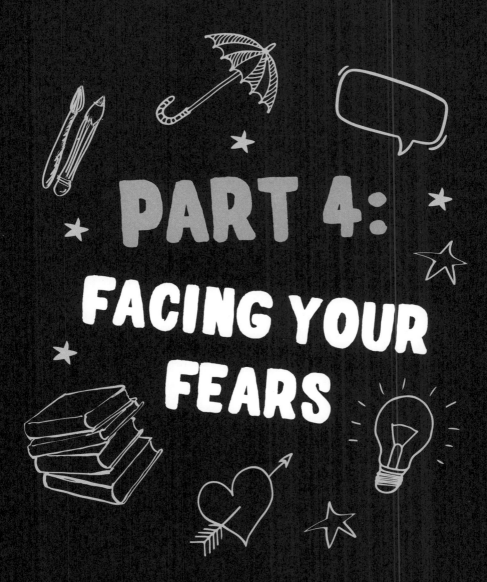

PART 4:

FACING YOUR FEARS

FEELING THE FEAR AND DOING IT ANYWAY

Ultimately, the way that anxiety can be beaten is by doing hard and anxiety-provoking things. When you face your fears, you will see that you can cope with more than you think, and your worries will become easier to deal with.

The truth is, you might never feel 100 per cent ready to try the things that make you feel anxious. Bravery isn't the absence of fear – it's doing things while you're still scared.

CREATING AN ACTION PLAN FOR WHEN ANXIETY STRIKES

Hopefully, you'll have picked up some useful tips and techniques already from the previous parts of this book. Now it's time to create a plan for when you start to feel anxious.

When you're feeling high anxiety, it can be difficult to think straight, so putting together a written plan when you're calm is a really helpful thing to do in preparation.

Pick and mix from these ideas, and add your own to the plan on the next page:

Take a break

Meditate

Sing

Log off

Take three deep breaths

Listen to my calming playlist

Say an affirmation

Go for a run

Put my hand on my heart

Do some yoga stretches

Go for a walk

Bounce on a trampoline

Write in my journal

Talk to someone

Take a bath

Have a glass of water

Use my weighted blanket

Have a snack

Check in with my five senses

When I feel anxious, I can...

STAY IN YOUR STRETCH ZONE

Facing your fears is really important... You can't beat anxiety without acting courageously. But it's also key to not overdo it.

Psychologists have developed a theory of three "zones" for anxiety.

* ★ **Your comfort zone is where you feel most calm – anxiety is low and things are predictable.**

* ★ **Your stretch zone is where you're challenging yourself – here is where you can face your fears. You feel anxious and uncomfortable but in control in your stretch zone.**

* ★ **The panic zone is where your body can no longer cope. Anxiety is too high and you feel totally overwhelmed.**

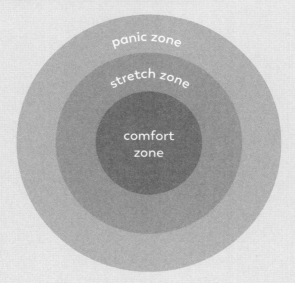

So it's good to go at your own pace. Slipping into the panic zone isn't a disaster but it can set you back and make facing your fears more difficult next time. When you're doing something that makes you feel anxious, take it slow and remember that it's OK to take breaks or try again another day.

TAKE YOUR TIME

It's important that you feel as in control as possible when you're doing the things that scare you, so it's OK to go at your own pace.

A great way of making sure you go at a speed that works for you is to break things down into steps, like a ladder to climb up. When you have small steps between you and something difficult, it makes it easier to get from where you are to where you want to be.

For many, the idea of asking someone out on a date is really anxiety-provoking. How could we break that down?

Ask your crush out on a date.

Text or talk to your crush to get to know them better.

Role-play with a friend – try switching roles!

Tell a friend about your problem.

Ask a friend to go for ice cream.

Rehearse in front of the mirror how to ask your crush out.

Remember: you don't have to climb upwards until you're ready, and it's OK to repeat steps or go backwards!

BREAK DOWN YOUR GOAL

Can you think of something that you'd like to do, but anxiety keeps getting in the way? Using the ladder idea from the last page, break down your goal into smaller steps to help you get to where you want to be:

YOU ARE BRAVE

If you're prone to anxiety, your mind needs to hear the message that you are brave and capable as often as possible. Your brain is like a forest floor, and the thoughts you have are paths across it. The more you think the same thought, the clearer and easier it becomes to walk that route. So it makes sense to practise thinking positive thoughts to create beautiful new paths in your mind.

Spend some time colouring in the affirmation on the facing page. Giving your attention to positive messages for a few minutes at a time will help your mind to absorb them, plus colouring is great for calming anxiety. When you begin to believe in yourself, you'll see that anxiety is not the boss of you.

I am
brave

HOPEFUL JOURNALING

At the start of each day, try visualizing the best possible outcome. You can do this every morning, especially when you've got a daunting or anxiety-provoking 24 hours ahead of you.

Think about how you'd like the day to go, what feelings you'd like to experience and what you'd like to achieve. Be hopeful but realistic – this isn't meant to make you feel inadequate or overburden you. Look at it more like a wish list for the day.

Give it a try here:

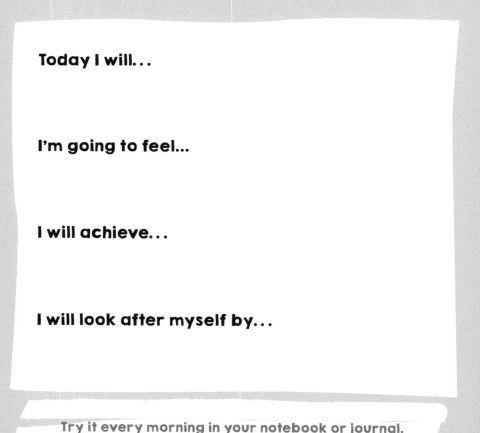

Today I will...

I'm going to feel...

I will achieve...

I will look after myself by...

Try it every morning in your notebook or journal.

EXPRESS YOUR FEELINGS

Naming how you are feeling is one of the bravest things you can do. When you're anxious, you don't need to pretend that it's not hard.

It can be good to practise some phrases to use when you're feeling worried, whether you're facing your fears or you're in a situation that's making you feel panic. That way you can concentrate on calming your body, rather than coming up with things to say.

Here are some ideas, with spaces to add your own...

Something about this is making me uncomfortable.

I need to take a break.

This is really hard.

I need some reassurance.

I'm feeling so anxious.

I need to leave now – I'll catch up with you later.

Can you help me break this down?

AT ONE POINT, YOU JUST LET GO AND GIVE YOURSELF TO YOUR LIFE. I HAVE FINALLY MANAGED THAT AND I GET SO MUCH MORE OUT OF LIFE.

Kristen Stewart

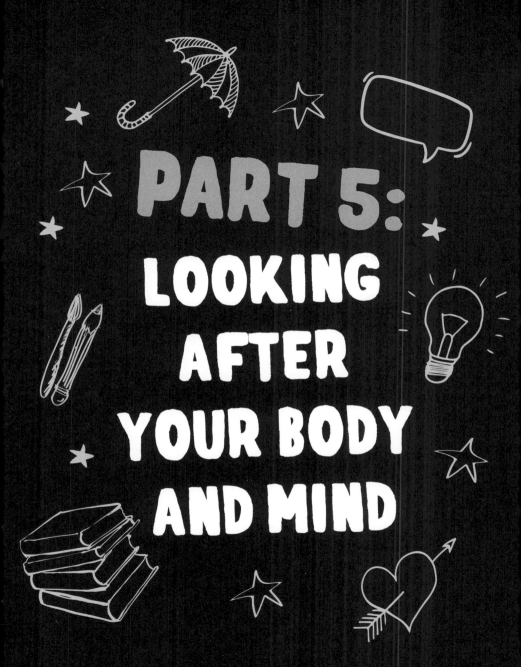

PART 5:
LOOKING AFTER YOUR BODY AND MIND

SELF-CARE AND ANXIETY

While anxiety is a normal, healthy emotion, research shows that the more you look after your body and mind, the more resilient you are and the faster you can bounce back from anxious moments.

Think about it – you're so much better-equipped to handle what life throws at you after a good night's sleep, a healthy meal and a good helping of downtime. Read on to find out how to take good care of yourself and minimize anxiety at the same time.

SOCIAL MEDIA

Social media is a brilliant tool for connecting and keeping in touch with others, finding out about the world, shopping, and expressing yourself. There are a lot of good things to be said for social media, but at the same time it can increase anxiety and have a negative effect on your mental health.

A study by the University of Pennsylvania found that reducing social media use to 30 minutes per day results in significantly lower levels of anxiety.

Have you ever felt anxious about social media? Perhaps you worry about how you come across or compare yourself to others online. Maybe you've been a victim of cyberbullying or seen it happen to someone else.

Next time you use social media, take a moment to pay attention to your mind and body. What thoughts are coming up for you? What sensations can you feel in your body? Just a few words for each is fine.

Before going on social media, I feel...

Anxiety level: /10

While I'm on social media, I feel...

Anxiety level:

After using social media, I feel...

Anxiety level: /10

MAKE YOUR FEED A POSITIVE PLACE TO BE

The internet has so much potential to inform, entertain and inspire us. But being connected to a whole world of content unfortunately means sometimes coming across things and people that make you anxious.

The great thing about the online world is that you can disengage quickly from what makes you feel worried, scared, controlled or bad about yourself. Blocking, unfriending, unfollowing and muting are tools that can be used on most websites and apps. There's often an option to report another user if they're behaving in a way that upsets you. When you stand up for yourself online, it benefits everyone, so don't be shy about using that block and report button.

Make sure your feed is filled with positive content that makes you feel safe and calm. Anything that makes you feel overwhelmed or anxious has got to go.

FEEL 5 PER CENT BETTER

Anxiety makes you feel awful. While it's not always possible to feel completely OK, you should generally be able to make yourself feel that little bit more comfortable, calm or reassured. At any moment in the day you can ask yourself:

What could I do to feel 5 per cent better?

That might involve positioning an extra cushion to sit more comfortably, taking a 10 minute break from studying or grabbing a glass of water.

What could you do right now to feel 5 per cent better?

FIND YOUR FLOW

Creativity is your mind's way of playing. Unlike other types of activity, there's no right or wrong way to be creative. This means it's an incredibly powerful way of calming anxiety, because there's no worrying about how it will turn out, only enjoying the process of creating. This is called "a state of flow" – when you're in the zone and just having fun.

Of course, it doesn't always feel that way. When you sit down to draw a picture and the result doesn't look like what you imagined, that doesn't feel good! The best anti-anxiety creative activities are ones that have no plan or expectations of what the outcome will be. Here are a few ideas to try:

Freehand drawing

Moving a pen or pencil any way you feel over paper. Let the pencil guide you and enjoy how the line moves, curves and gets lighter or darker.

Dance

Put on a high-energy song and dance your heart out.

Blob creatures

Make a random blob shape using pen, pencil or paint. Now draw an outline around it, and give it eyes, legs, accessories and anything else you can think of to make it into a creature.

Stream of consciousness writing

Write whatever's in your mind onto paper. Don't worry about spellings, grammar or even making sense!

Found poetry

Look around you to find words and phrases that grab your attention and make them into a poem – try this on the next page...

MAKE A FOUND POEM

You will need: paper, pen, scissors and glue/tape

Walk around your room, house or local neighbourhood, and keep your eyes and ears open for words and phrases. They might be written down, printed, on a screen or said aloud. When you find something that gets your attention, write it on a piece of paper. Keep going until you have 10–15 different snippets of text.

Now carefully cut out each line of text and play around with them. You can add or take away words – it's totally up to you. See if any of the lines go together to tell an interesting or weird story, or just put them in a random order that feels right.

Good sources for found poetry:

Opening a book at a random page

Songs on the radio

Overheard conversations

Newspaper headlines

Social media posts

Advertising posters

Food packaging

When you're happy with your found poem, stick your pieces of paper here:

YOU ARE THE SKY. EVERYTHING ELSE — IT'S JUST THE WEATHER.

Pema Chödrön

BE KIND TO YOURSELF

Studies have found that the voice you use to speak to yourself is one of the biggest influences on your mental well-being. Those who have a kind and patient inner voice are able to comfort themselves in times of worry, stress or sadness. If yours is less like a best friend and more like a bully or a strict teacher, you'll find it harder to get unstuck from negative emotions.

The good news is, you can make your inner voice kinder. It takes practice, but you can do it. The first step is to recognize when your inner voice is talking.

Think back to a time when you felt anxious or overwhelmed. How do you feel about that past version of yourself, when you felt so anxious? Write it down here:

The things you've written should give you a good idea of your inner voice: yours is a positive one if you've voiced kind words. However, if your inner voice is unkind and makes you feel ashamed for having struggled in the past, you could do with showing yourself a little more compassion.

What could you say to the anxious, past version of yourself that would be more supportive?

BE KIND TO YOURSELF MIND-HACK

One quick trick to help you build a kinder inner voice is to imagine that you are talking to your best friend – be just as patient, kind and encouraging as you would be to them. Speak to yourself as if you were two separate people, like this:

What if I fail... Oh my god, I can't do this!

I believe in you — you can do this.

But I'm soooo scared...

You're just feeling anxious about this — it's OK to feel anxious.

I'm going to run and hide in my bed.

This is really hard, but you can do hard things.

Research has found that the more distance we can create between ourselves and our emotions, the easier it is to deal with them. Talking to your anxious mind as if you were two different people will make those overwhelming feelings seem that bit further away from you.

YOU ARE UNIQUE

Do you ever feel anxious about how you look? It's a common cause of anxiety among teens. Your body and those of your friends are changing, and it can feel like you're going too slow or too fast compared to everyone else.

Remember that you are unique. There is no need for you to grow at the same rate as those around you, to look like everyone else or to be into the same things. It's OK to simply be yourself.

If you feel worried or unsure about any aspect of puberty or your body, you can always talk to a trusted adult about it.

GROW YOUR SELF-LOVE

Learning to love and trust your mind and body is the greatest gift you can give yourself, as well as one of the strongest ways to fight anxiety. Try this self-love gratitude exercise to remind yourself why you're amazing.

I'm grateful to my body for...

I'm grateful to my mind for...

I'm grateful to be good at...

I'll always remember receiving this compliment...

EXERCISING TO REDUCE ANXIETY

All kinds of physical exercise help to reduce anxiety, from walking to team sports, dance classes to boxing.

Movement contributes to freeing our minds from anxious thoughts, by bringing our focus and attention into our bodies. When we move, we release tension and energy, and we calm our emotions (see page 39).

So it makes sense to build exercise and movement into your daily routine. Even if you only manage 10 minutes a day, it will help to regulate your emotions and calm anxiety.

Try cycling to get you around or a team sport for the social benefits.

Having a goal to aim for is a good idea – how about Couch to 5K or a swimming challenge?

The most important thing is to choose something you enjoy, as motivation plays a huge part when sticking to a routine.

Have a think about your daily and weekly schedule – jot it down here and see where you can fit some exercise in each day:

Sunday	
Saturday	
Friday	
Thursday	
Wednesday	
Tuesday	
Monday	

EAT WELL

Ever felt hangry? How about hanxious? It's a thing! When you go too long without food, your blood glucose levels drop, and your body releases hormones to keep you going. These hormones have a powerful effect on your emotions, meaning you're more easily tipped over into big feelings of anger, sadness or anxiety.

So next time you feel anxiety building up, check in with your stomach – are you hungry or thirsty? If so, grab a healthy snack or drink and you'll notice your anxiety become a little more manageable.

Best anti-anxiety snacks

Look for snacks that are high in vitamins and release energy slowly – these will help you to avoid hanxiety-inducing blood-glucose crashes.

★ **Probiotic yoghurt**

★ **Berries**

★ **Almonds**

★ **Guacamole**

★ **Wholewheat crackers**

★ **Toast with peanut butter and sliced banana**

If you drink coffee, it might be time to cut down! The high caffeine content can make anxiety worse because it makes your heart beat faster, speeds up your breathing and dehydrates the body. Switch to green tea if you're looking for a gentler caffeine boost.

SLEEP WELL

The better you sleep, the more in control of your emotions you'll be while you're awake. But this can be really hard to achieve if anxiety makes it hard for you to get some rest.

On top of this, puberty causes your circadian rhythm (when your body feels like sleeping and waking up) to shift to a couple of hours later, meaning that your sleep habits can be irregular and slightly out of step with the rest of your family's.

A really good night-time routine is the best way to ensure that getting to sleep becomes as straightforward as possible. Turn off all screens at least an hour before you plan to go to bed – the blue-tinged light can disrupt your circadian rhythm – and do something enjoyable and relaxing like taking a bath, writing in a journal or reading a chapter of a book. It's less about the activity and more about getting used to doing the same relaxing things each night – forming a habit means that your body will pick up on the signals that it's time to wind down each evening.

What's your night-time routine?

BEDTIME BODY SCAN

If you find yourself getting anxious when you're trying to get to sleep, you're not alone. Many people struggle with this, and there's no one-size-fits-all solution. Try this mindful body scan as part of your night-time routine to help you relax and rest.

Lie in bed and close your eyes. Breathe freely. Begin by thinking about the top of your head. Move slowly down, one body part at a time, checking whether any of them are feeling tense and relaxing those that are. Imagine your body softening into the warmth of your bed. Keep going, slowly, until you reach your toes and relax all of them, one by one.

You might start to feel bored while doing a body scan... that just means it's working! You can't fall asleep while your mind is spinning or concentrating on something entertaining, so let yourself feel bored.

STAY HYDRATED

Just like those times when you don't get enough sleep or food, not having enough water in your body can make your anxiety worse. A dry mouth, racing heart and feeling too hot can be caused by dehydration or anxiety – their signs are very similar.

It won't solve any real-life problems, but having a glass of fresh water will help to calm your anxiety and make you feel that little bit more in control when you're having a hard time. Better still, getting in the habit of having a bottle of water with you all the time, and sipping from it regularly, will mean that you're always hydrated.

Aim for 2 litres of water a day – that's approximately eight tall glasses.

GET INTO NATURE

Being outside has been proven to lower anxiety. Even if it's raining, the combination of fresh air, gentle exercise and natural light will have an instant effect on your mood.

Try to get outside every day. Green spaces are best – like a local park, forest, beach or riverbank.

Can you picture a really calming natural place? It could be from your imagination or somewhere you know well. Draw it here:

SOOTHING SELF-CARE

Beyond taking care of your basic needs, self-care can also be about soothing yourself when you're feeling anxious.

Using your senses to bring yourself comfort will help to calm your body and slow racing thoughts. Here are some ideas for soothing self-care:

Sight

Watch a feel-good TV show, read a book, watch the world go by

Smell

Have a bath with a scented bath bomb, play with some scented putty, do some baking

Touch

Wrap yourself in a soft blanket, hug someone you love, play with a stress ball

Sound

Listen to soothing music, sing to yourself, follow a guided meditation

Taste

Eat mindfully, drink hot chocolate, chew gum

MAKE A SELF-SOOTHE BOX

Keeping some of the things that can comfort you together in a box or bag will mean they're easier to find when you need them.

Use the space here to brainstorm ideas of what could go in your self-soothe box...

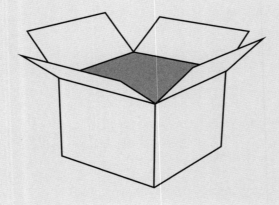

Here are some suggestions to get you started:

Fidget toy

Photos of cute animals

A note from your bestie

Favourite comfy sweater

Feel-good movie

Book of positive quotes

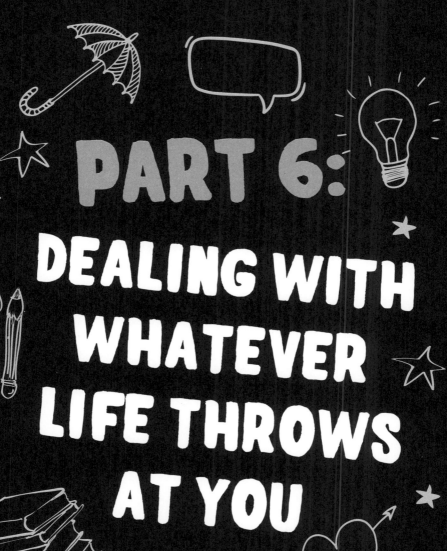

PART 6:
DEALING WITH WHATEVER LIFE THROWS AT YOU

BE PREPARED FOR CURVEBALLS

Whether it's exams, family, friends or relationships, unexpected things will happen and you'll face challenges that'll make you feel anxious. Planning ahead and making sure you have tried-and-tested techniques for calming yourself will help you to feel more in control and capable, whatever happens.

ANXIETY HACKS

When you've got something coming up, like exams, that's making you anxious but you need to be ready for, try these anxiety hacks. They might feel like the opposite of what you want to do, and that's the clever part – when you go against what anxiety is telling you to do, you outsmart it!

Do the hard stuff first

Don't put off the trickiest subjects: do them in small chunks alongside something easier. Try setting a timer for 20 minutes – do the dreaded task until time's up, then take a break.

Do it together

Ask a friend or family member to study, prepare with or even do a "dry run" together. Anxiety hates company, and speaking about your worries often makes them feel a lot more manageable.

No cramming!

Leaving revision, study or preparation until the last minute is a recipe for stress and anxiety. Break your tasks down well in advance so you can do a little bit every day – you could use the break-it-down planner on page 117 to help you or the be-prepared planner on page 112, if you feel overwhelmed.

The shakedown

When you get stuck in your head – finding yourself zoning out or caught up with anxious thoughts – it helps to literally shake yourself out of it. Stand up, sweep your arms up and down, run on the spot, shake your hips, and get all that nervous energy out of your body. Now you're ready to begin.

Turn off notifications

If you find yourself getting distracted by notifications or tempting apps, put your phone on silent while you're studying. Apps like Freedom and Forest can help you to focus by blocking distracting content.

BE-PREPARED PLANNER

Try this be-prepared planner for when you're stuck in a situation that makes you feel anxious. Sitting down to think about things clearly and getting them down on paper can help you to feel more in control. You can write down all the ideas, solutions, thoughts and feelings that you come up with, and pick the ones that you think will work best.

Here's one already filled out:

What's happening?
My friend lent me her jacket and I've spilled paint on it.

How do I feel? What am I thinking?
Panic, anxiety. I'll have to buy her a new jacket but I don't have enough money. I'll get in trouble and lose a friend.

How big is the problem?

I   2   3   4   (5)   6   7   8   q   10

What can I do to feel better right now?
Take some deep breaths.
Ask for help.

What can I do to solve the problem right now?
Try to wash the paint out.

Who can help me with this?
Dad or Mum.

What can I do to solve the problem this week?
Return the jacket once it has been cleaned and be honest about what happened.

What did I learn from this?
That mistakes can be put right (Dad knew how to get paint out of denim) and that my friend forgave me. I'll be more careful with other people's stuff next time.

Try it yourself next time you're feeling anxious:

What's happening?

How do I feel? What am I thinking?

How big is the problem?
1   2   3   4   5   6   7   8   9   10

What can I do to feel better right now?

What can I do to solve the problem right now?

Who can help me with this?

What can I do to solve the problem this week?

What did I learn from this?

TALK ABOUT IT

Being anxious might feel embarrassing and something that should be hidden away from others. In reality, it's OK to find things difficult, and talking about it helps to lessen anxiety.

Research shows that discussing our feelings can have an instant, positive effect on our emotions – making anxiety, pain, sadness and anger less intense. This could be because naming our emotions activates the right side of the brain, so the effect of the amygdala on our thoughts and feelings is reduced.

Talk to someone you're close to and trust – it might feel like your anxiety is very obvious to others, but often people can't see it unless you tell them. Most importantly, be gentle with yourself and know that there are people who care about you and want to help.

If talking face-to-face feels too much, try writing a letter, email or text instead.

There are lots of people you can talk to, not just those in your immediate family. Teachers, aunts and uncles, family friends or other trusted adults will want to be there for you and hear about your feelings. You can also ask to talk to your doctor or a therapist about anxiety.

When you speak to someone, tell them whether you would like them just to listen or if you are looking for advice. This will help them support you.

VISUALIZATION

Your imagination is a powerful thing. Scientists have found that imagining doing something stimulates the same parts of your brain as actually doing it. So when you picture things going well, it's like practice for your brain – you'll subconsciously start to expect a good outcome.

Athletes use visualization to help them run races in their goal times. They picture themselves achieving their aim and this has been proven to make it more likely to happen.

Next time you're feeling anxious about something, imagine it going well. Close your eyes and focus your attention on your visualization. Give the picture you imagine as much detail as possible – what can you see, hear, smell, feel and taste? Imagine what could happen step-by-step.

Sketch your visualization here:

BREAKING IT DOWN

Some things can feel huge and overwhelming to think about, like revising for an exam. Sometimes it feels easier to put it off for another day and hide under the covers. This is called procrastination, and it's a common sign of anxiety.

The hardest part about procrastination is that the longer you put off beginning something, the bigger a problem it becomes, especially in the case of something like exam revision, where there's a deadline. Knowing this doesn't usually make it any easier, though!

Procrastination

Noun

The action of delaying or postponing something.

If you catch yourself procrastinating because of anxiety, don't be too hard on yourself. One great way of beating this cycle is to break tasks down into smaller pieces. That way, you're faced with a number of manageable jobs to complete one at a time, rather than a huge mountain of work.

Try using the planner on the next page to help you.

WEEKLY PLANNER

WEEKLY GOALS	MONDAY

TUESDAY	WEDNESDAY	THURSDAY

FRIDAY	SATURDAY	SUNDAY

Top priorities

1.

2.

3.

Who can be there for me this week?

Self-care:

Would love to do:

Have to do:

MAKE YOUR ROOM A CALM ZONE

Having a corner that's just yours – whether that's your bedroom or your own bed – will help you to deal with life's ups and downs. Taking good care of your space and making sure it's a calm, relaxing place to be means there's always somewhere you can go to wind down.

Try these tips to make your own chill-out zone:

Stick wrapping paper, pictures from magazines or fabric with a calming pattern on your wall – blues and purples work well, as do images from space or nature.

Get some earphones so you can tune out the noise of the world for a while. Make a calming playlist to plug into whenever you need.

Invest in some string lights for a soft, sleepy glow while you wind down.

Succulent plants are easy to care for and great to look at. They even improve the air quality in your room, giving you a better night's sleep.

Keep a notebook by your bed for journaling away anxious thoughts.

Stick affirmations and inspiring quotes on your wall, using Post-its.

Spend a little time tidying up every day – make your bed, and open the curtains nice and wide. It doesn't need to be perfect, but it's so much easier to relax in an organized space rather than a cluttered one.

A JOURNEY OF A THOUSAND MILES BEGINS WITH A SINGLE STEP.

Lao Tzu

PART 7:

FRIENDSHIPS
AND
RELATIONSHIPS

BEING YOURSELF

The relationships we have with other people can be a big source of anxiety. When you worry about what others think of you or how they react to you, it can be hard to relax and be yourself. If there's an argument or conflict, it becomes even harder. In this chapter we'll look at strategies for managing anxiety in your family, friendships and relationships.

COMPARING YOURSELF TO OTHERS

Comparing yourself to other people is almost always a bad idea. It's bad for your self-esteem and can leave you feeling anxious that you need to change in order to measure up.

It also steers your attention away from the positive things in your life and your achievements. It's important to find a balance between challenging yourself and appreciating yourself as you are.

So how can you stop comparing? The key is to get comfortable with not knowing. As anxiety wants to create a story and know every detail, it will have you making assumptions about other people. For example, you might assume that your friend who gets 100 per cent in every test finds it easy and doesn't need to revise. The truth could be quite different!

By taking a moment to pause and remind yourself that you don't know anyone else's full story, you give yourself the chance to see the many alternative scenarios that are possible, and this makes it easier to stop comparing yourself.

> **Try this: take a deep breath and say:**
> **"I am OK exactly as I am."**

BOUNDARIES

What are boundaries? They're the limits of what you're OK with. "I don't answer texts after 9 p.m." is an example of a boundary. "I'm free next week, but not before" is another, and so is: "I'm not ready for that – it makes me feel really anxious".

Even though boundaries can help to keep us out of uncomfortable situations, communicating them can be a huge source of anxiety. You might worry about hurting someone else's feelings or even losing a friendship.

If that sounds like you, it helps to be prepared. For example, if you're going to a party where you know that the host might want you to stay later than you're comfortable with, decide what time you want to leave beforehand. You could even let the host know in advance.

People who care about you will understand and welcome your clarity about your limits.

Here are some useful boundary-setting phrases to get comfortable with:

No.

That's not going to work for me.

I'd love to stay, but I have to go now.

That's all I can offer.

Sorry, I can't.

Stop, I don't like that.

Something about this feels uncomfortable.

While communicating boundaries clearly is a really great skill to master, sometimes it's not practical. You can communicate discomfort by using body language – or simply leave if you ever feel in danger.

OPEN UP

Being open about anxiety is one of the bravest and hardest things you can do. It's also one of the most empowering. Do you know someone you'd feel comfortable sharing your feelings with?

Write a list of the people in your life who could listen to you. What makes each of them a good listener?

If you don't have someone you'd feel OK talking to, check the resources on page 140 – you're not alone and there is help available.

WHAT MAKES A GOOD FRIENDSHIP OR RELATIONSHIP? AND WHAT MAKES A BAD ONE?

Romantically involved or just friends, there are certain qualities that will help you determine whether someone is a good fit for you.

Positive	Negative
Lets you be yourself	Puts you down for who you are
Is fine with you having other friends	Controls who you see
Replies to your messages	Ignores or ghosts you
Is considerate of your feelings	Treats you like your feelings don't matter
Is interested in your thoughts, feelings and experiences	Only talks about what interests them
Makes you feel safe	Makes you feel anxious or unsafe
Laughs with you	Laughs at you
You can tell them if they've upset you	Refuses to acknowledge that they've upset you
Accepts "no"	Gets angry or manipulative when told "no"
They want to hang out with you	They will drop you for other plans

WHAT TO DO IF YOU ARE IN A BAD FRIENDSHIP OR RELATIONSHIP

If you're in a friendship or relationship where you feel unsafe or unable to leave, it's not your fault. This can happen to anyone and the blame lies solely with the person who is treating you disrespectfully. They might use guilt or threats to stop you from leaving, and suffering with anxiety could make this even harder for you to deal with.

Remember: you are entitled to put your comfort and safety first, and you are not responsible for other people's emotions.

There are many people you can talk to if you're unsure about someone in your life or want confidential advice. Think of an adult that you know and trust. Then check out page 140 for more resources. You're not alone and you deserve to be treated with respect.

MANAGING EXPECTATIONS

It might feel like there are a lot of expectations on you right now. Pressure to do well at school, have perfect skin, pass exams, plan your future, get a boyfriend or girlfriend... argh! When you're under pressure, anxiety about not measuring up to these expectations can make things extra hard to deal with.

What pressure or expectations do you feel from parents, friends, school, the media or other sources? Write about them here:

Sometimes a bit of healthy expectation can motivate you, even if it's pretty annoying – like when your parents tell you to put down your phone and do your homework... It can help you to focus and fulfil your potential. But mostly, pressures from outside sources aren't helpful – like the expectation to look a certain way – and will make you feel anxious about not fitting in or having to change who you are.

Which expectations are helpful to you?

Which expectations are unhelpful to you?
What would it be like to let go of them?

Can you use one of the affirmations from this book, or one you've made up yourself, to help you think about one of these expectations differently? For example, if you feel anxious about your body looking different to other people's, you might say to yourself: "I am OK exactly as I am" or "I am more than just my body".

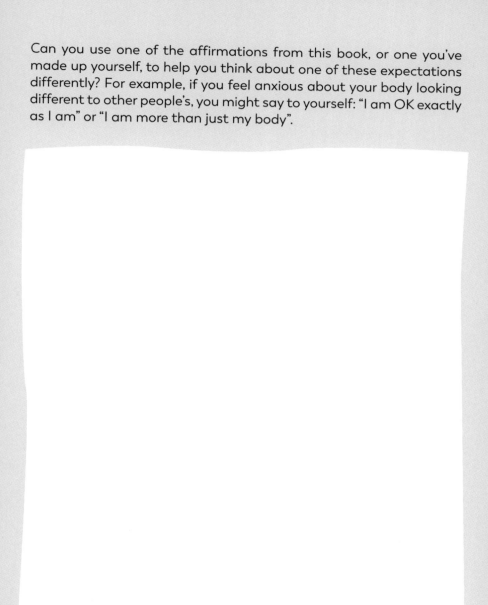

While we can't control other people's expectations, we can influence how we think and feel about them, and how much we allow them to bother us.

MAKE A "POSITIVELY ME" JAR

You are strong and there is only one you in the whole world. Feeling good about yourself is at the heart of tackling anxiety, as that's when you know that you can trust yourself to cope, whatever happens.

Collecting little reminders of things that fill you up with good feelings in a "positively me" jar is a great way to boost your positivity whenever necessary.

You will need:
A clean, empty jar
Small pieces or scraps of paper
Stickers and paint pens (optional)

Take your small pieces of paper and, on them, write compliments, good things that have happened to you, occasions when you were kind or generous, achievements, jokes, things you love about yourself, happy memories... anything that makes you smile!

Fold the pieces of paper and place them inside the jar.

Use stickers and paint pens to decorate your jar – let it reflect your personality.

Every time you think of something new that makes you smile, write it down and add it to your jar.

Every time you feel anxious and need to lift your mood, grab your jar for an instant boost.

Bonus tip: get your bestie to write some things to go in your jar!

YOU ARE MORE PRECIOUS TO THIS WORLD THAN YOU'LL EVER KNOW.

Lili Reinhart

PART 8:

LOOKING
FORWARD

A BRIGHT FUTURE

Anxiety can make the future seem like a dark and negative place, but it doesn't have to be that way. Using the tools you've learned and your inner strength, you can look forward to a bright and positive future, knowing that you can count on yourself to cope and reach out for help when you need it. In this final section, we'll look at how you can use the things you've learned in this book as part of your everyday life.

MY ANXIETY FIRST-AID KIT

When you're feeling anxious, it can be hard to remember what helps. Jot down the things that work for you here, so you can return to this page any time you feel anxious and need some help calming down quickly.

I can talk to...

An idea that helps me...
(e.g. I can take this one breath at a time)

An activity that helps me...
(e.g. colouring)

Remember that...
(e.g. I can't control everything)

A movie that makes me feel good...

A song that calms me...

How long since I had a snack or drank a glass of water?

VISUALIZE A CALMER YOU

Take some time to visualize your life as you would like it to be, using your emotions and all five of your senses. Picture yourself calm and confident, achieving your goals and chasing your dreams.

What kind of images come up? What do you see yourself doing, wearing, eating? Where do you see yourself living or travelling to?

Try making a mood board of what your best life would look like. Save images to a visualization folder, use Pinterest or make an old-fashioned collage out of cut-out pictures from magazines.

YOU'RE NOT ALONE

Most young people will struggle with anxious feelings at some point – you're far from alone. Here are a few teens who've been through hard times and learned ways to conquer anxiety.

When my parents split up, I was so worried that I'd done something to cause it. I tried to be perfect but I couldn't sleep because I was always thinking of ways I could be an even better daughter. One day I couldn't take it any more – I broke down in tears and told my mum everything. She and Dad have helped me understand that it wasn't my fault, and that they both love me just as I am. It's hard, but I'm learning to like my new life.

Matilda, 14

I was off school for almost a year because I was ill. I was so happy when the doctors told me I was well enough to go back, but when I actually got into the classroom, I was so anxious I couldn't even speak. Everyone had changed while I was away. My form tutor noticed that I was struggling and, together with my parents and old friends, he helped me to feel comfortable in school again.

George, 12

When I got really anxious, I used to lash out at others. I said and did some really hurtful things that I regret. My dad signed me up for a karate class, and it's really helped me deal with anger and cope with anxiety in a healthier way.

Ed, 14

When I started my period, I was so paranoid that my pad would leak and everyone would know. I used to wear one every day, even when I wasn't bleeding, and constantly check my clothes. Learning more about my body, and understanding that menstruation is normal and natural rather than shameful, means that I feel a lot more comfortable with my changing body now. If someone knows I'm on my period, so what?

Caomihe, 16

ASK FOR HELP

If you're struggling with anxiety, or any other aspect of mental health, there are lots of organizations out there that can provide help and advice. If you feel like your anxiety is starting to affect your life, it's a good idea to talk with an adult you trust and make an appointment with a doctor.

Anxiety in Teens
0330 606 1174
www.anxietyinteens.org
Resources to equip young adults in the US with tools and community to advance emotional wellness.

Anxiety UK
03444 775 774 (helpline)
07537 416 905 (text)
www.anxietyuk.org.uk
Advice and support for people living with anxiety.

BEAT
0808 801 0711
www.beateatingdisorders.co.uk
Under-18s helpline, webchat and online support groups for people with eating disorders, such as anorexia and bulimia.

Campaign Against Living Miserably (CALM)
0800 58 58 58
www.thecalmzone.net
Provides listening services, information and support, including a webchat, for anyone who needs to talk.

Childline
0800 1111
www.childline.org.uk
Support for young people in the UK, including a free 24-hour helpline.

FRANK
0300 123 6600
www.talktofrank.com
Confidential advice and information about drugs, their effects and the law.

The Jed Foundation
1 800 273 8255
www.jedfoundation.org
Information and advice for US
teens to promote emotional and
mental health.

On My Mind
020 7794 2313
www.annafreud.org/on-my-mind
Information for young people to
make informed choices about
their mental health and well-
being.

Refuge
0808 2000 247
www.refuge.org.uk
Advice about domestic abuse and
support for those affected by it.

Young Minds
0808 802 5544
www.youngminds.org.uk
Information about every aspect
of mental well-being for young
people.

FURTHER READING

Check out these books for teens about anxiety, mental health and
building resilience:

The 10pm Question
Kate De Goldi

The Teenage Guide to Stress
Nicola Morgan

The Wind Singer
William Nicholson

*Put Your Worries Here: A Creative
Journal for Teens with Anxiety*
Lisa Schab

*The Shyness and Social Anxiety
Workbook for Teens*
Jennifer Shannon

The Confidence Code for Girls
Claire Shipman and Katty Kay

*The Self-Care Kit for Stressed-Out
Teens*
Frankie Young

CONCLUSION

You can trust yourself, even when you feel full of anxiety. You are brave and strong, even when you feel scared and alone. Learning to overcome anxiety is hard work, and it's OK to take your time. Going at your own pace is what will build resilience and trust in yourself.

I hope you've found some useful ideas and strategies in this book. Remember that you can cope with whatever life throws at you and that you are never alone – you can reach out for help and people will be there for you. Anxiety is a part of being human, but it doesn't have to control your life. You have the power to be positively you, no matter what.

YOU'VE GOT THIS!

Paperback

£10.99

978-1-78685-801-6

Do you often feel you're not good enough?

Your teens are full of new challenges – exams, peer pressure, planning your future and anything and everything in between. This can turn every day into a minefield of emotions and lead to one big headache. How you feel about yourself in all this chaos can make life even tougher. When you think you don't measure up, it can be hard to pick yourself up again, but when you feel good about yourself, you can approach every situation with confidence and say "I've got this!" This book contains top tips and activities to help your self-esteem flourish and make you proud to be awesomely you.

If you're interested in finding out more about our books, find us on Facebook at **Summersdale Publishers**, on Twitter at **@Summersdale** and on Instagram at **@summersdalebooks**.

www.summersdale.com

IMAGE CREDITS

Cover, inside cover and title page images: girl © pimchawee/Shutterstock.com; hearts © Karolina Madej/Shutterstock.com; pizza © Angelina De Sol/Shutterstock.com; laptop © pimchawee/Shutterstock.com; hand holding phone © pimchawee/Shutterstock.com; clock, earth, star outline, pencil, brush © icon0.com/Shutterstock.com; heart with arrow © Kseniia Bakshaeva/Shutterstock.com; boy © IRINA SHI/Shutterstock.com; bulb, umbrella © Kseniia Bakshaeva/Shutterstock.com; stack of books © Ohn Mar/Shutterstock.com

Brain characters throughout © Illustratio/Shutterstock.com
pp.33, 34 – brain © maglyvi/Shutterstock.com
p.81 – colouring page © ComPix/Shutterstock.com
p.137 – pinboard © Sulee7824/Shutterstock.com